THE
BRITISH SOLDIER
OF THE
SECOND WORLD WAR

Peter Doyle

SHIRE PUBLICATIONS

First published in Great Britain in 2009 by Shire
Publications Ltd, Midland House, West Way, Botley,
Oxford OX2 0PH, United Kingdom.
443 Park Avenue South, New York, NY 10016, USA.

E-mail: shire@shirebooks.co.uk   www.shirebooks.co.uk

A CIP catalogue record for this book is available from the
British Library.

Shire Library no. 569   •   ISBN-13: 978 0 7478 0741 4

Peter Doyle has asserted his right under the Copyright,
Designs and Patents Act, 1988, to be identified as the
author of this book.

Designed by Ken Vail Graphic Design, Cambridge, UK and
typeset in Perpetua and Gill Sans.
Printed in Malta by Gutenberg Press Ltd.

09 10 11 12 13   10 9 8 7 6 5 4 3 2 1

COVER IMAGE
A stoic and optimistic view of the British soldier from a
children's book of 1939.

TITLE PAGE IMAGE
Gunner Howard Daniel of the Royal Artillery wears a
standard aertex shirt with slip-overs bearing the insignia of
the 56th Infantry Division. Serving with the 8th Army, he
was awarded the Africa Star, before being part of the
invasion force that landed in Italy.

CONTENTS PAGE IMAGE
Jon's 'Two Types' were popular cartoon characters, their
eccentric dress code typifying that of the soldiers of the
8th Army.

ACKNOWLEDGEMENTS

The Trustees of the Imperial War Museum are thanked for
permission to publish the photographs on pages 4, 16, 26,
31, 36, 41, 46, 50. I am grateful to the following people
who have helped in providing information or materials for
this book: Richard Archer, Guy Baldwin, Bella Bennett,
Paul Evans, Donald and Vernon Fletcher, Adam Forster,
Steve Morris, Billy Simpson, Libby Simpson and Tom
Stafford. I thank Julie and James for their love and support

IMPERIAL WAR MUSEUM COLLECTIONS

Several of the photos in this book come from the Imperial
War Museum's huge collections, which cover all aspects of
conflict involving Britain and the Commonwealth since the
start of the twentieth century. These rich resources are
available online to search, browse and buy at
www.iwmcollections.org.uk. In addition to Collections
Online, you can visit the Visitor Rooms where you can
explore over 8 million photographs, thousands of hours of
moving images, the largest sound archive of its kind in the
world, thousands of diaries and letters written by people
in wartime, and a huge reference library. To make an
appointment, call (020) 7416 5320, or e-mail
mail@iwm.org.uk. Imperial War Museum
www.iwm.org.uk

CONTENTS

'UNPREPARED', 1939–41

THE EFFORTS of the British soldiers of 1939–45 have been overshadowed by the overwhelming numerical superiority of their main allies, the Americans. Yet the British served across the world, in theatres stretching from northern Europe to the Far East, and would lose over 300,000 men; they would stand alone against Nazi Germany in 1940, and be in the vanguard of victory in 1945. The purpose of this short book is to focus on the British soldier in order to help family historians understand the wartime lives of their family members in this most global of all wars. Although it cannot hope to be comprehensive, it sets out the main theatres in which the British soldier served during six long years of war, and describes his uniforms, equipment and operations.

At the close of 1918, the British Army could argue legitimately that it was one of the strongest forces ever assembled. With five million men under arms, new weaponry including tanks, ground attack aircraft and artillery tactics, the British Army was in the vanguard of the force that defeated Imperial Germany. But that ascendancy was not to be maintained; with almost a million dead, and two million more physically or psychologically damaged by the experience, there was no way that this titanic level of commitment could be maintained. Year on year in the inter-war period, successive governments cut back on defence spending, and the armed forces lapsed into their traditional peacetime mode of Imperial commitment and decadent swagger. The army was to stagnate through the years of indifference in the post-war politics of appeasement and defensiveness.

There were some thinkers still. Britain had invented tank warfare, and through the 'learning curve' of experience on the Western Front had pioneered the use of tanks as a battle-winning force. Mechanisation of a modern army was clearly the way forward; tanks replacing cavalry, troop transports (in the form of lorries and carriers) replacing the footslogging march of the infantry. Children's books from the period celebrate this daringly modern development. It also meant that the planners could pare back the troop numbers – would not a mechanised force have greater impact on the battlefield?

Opposite:
Men rescued from the beaches of Dunkirk on their way home.
(IWM C 1750)

Territorial soldiers at a training camp in 1937; Britain's armed forces would be woefully under-prepared for the coming war.

A children's book from 1939. Hopelessly optimistic, books like this extolled the virtues of the modern, mechanised British Army.

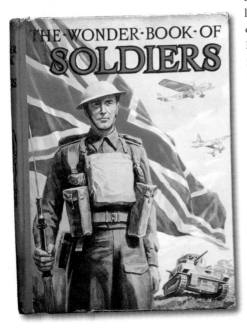

Yet, despite the fine intentions, the development of the tank was largely left to others as the British dallied with ponderous infantry tanks or under-gunned scouts with hopeless armour – both incapable of taking on an enemy armed with more aggressively equipped fighting vehicles. And, while France commenced the construction of the monumental linear fortress that was meant to secure its eastern boundaries from German aggression, Britain reduced its army to a level of 200,000 men, and contented itself with a policy that no longer saw its once defeated enemy as a future aggressor. This policy was to change with the rise of Adolf Hitler in a Germany weakened by economic depression. By the mid 1930s the threat was clear and present; and with appeasement came also the desperate need to rearm and re-equip, a need that was thrown into sharp relief by the Munich Crisis of September 1938. From this point onwards the British could no longer afford to be complacent, and a new urgency was to arise.

The British Army of 1939 was a shadow of its former self, and could not even draw comfort from the fact that the army of 1914 was of a similar scale. The army of 1914 was highly trained, well equipped and highly motivated; none of these attributes would apply in 1939. Only four regular army battalions could be mobilised to meet the threat of war following the rise of Hitler. Voluntary National Service had first been announced by Prime Minister Neville Chamberlain in 1938, but with the growing German threat in 1938–9, the Government had reacted – with some reticence – to try to counter that threat by finally instigating conscription in April 1939. At the very least, the Government hoped to prevent a repeat of the volunteer culture of 1914, when the 'flower of British youth' had joined the colours in droves, leaving behind industry and commerce to struggle in supplying the war. For the sake of the nation, this could not afford to be repeated in a new war. Men who reached the age of twenty were thus conscripted into the Territorial Army (TA) with the freshly re-minted title of 'Militia'. This doubled the size of the TA, but increased dramatically the number of partially trained troops draining the nation of military resources, uniforms and equipment. At the outbreak of war, all distinctions would be swept aside, and all men would simply become embodied into the British Army.

With the Territorial Army doubled on the eve of war, these cigarette cards were issued to celebrate their achievements – and advertise their preparedness.

The Royal Armoured Corps was formed in April 1939 in order to encompass the renamed Royal Tank Regiment and the mechanised cavalry regiments. Most cavalry regiments were integrated into the Corps, and new armoured 'cavalry' units would also be raised during the war, none of which would ever ride horses into battle. All would wear a distinctive black beret (including, later in the war, General Montgomery, with his famous dual-badged version). British tank strength was pitiful: in 1936, there were only 375 armoured vehicles in British service. With the need to rearm a growing imperative, this was to rise to around 2,000 at the outbreak of war.

The 'Phoney War' was the phrase given by American journalists to the period between Britain's declaration of war in September 1939 (following Germany's assault on Poland) and the launching of *Fall Gelb*, the Nazi Blitzkrieg campaign in the west, opened in May 1940. Incomplete in its northern sector, facing neutral Belgium, the Maginot Line was France's answer to the threat from the east. Reliant on the difficult terrain of the Ardennes forest in

The black beret of the Royal Armoured Corps, worn by all ranks.

the south and on Belgian resolve to defend their own neutrality in the north, the French were content to sit behind their fortress and wait. The British Expeditionary Force (BEF) of 1939 was deployed much as it had been in 1914, adjacent to the Belgian border. Prevented from entering this neutral country, the BEF had little choice but to prepare its own positions; trenches were once again dug, and patrols were sent out into a new no man's land. While the British soldiers in France were aware of the brooding presence of their German counterparts behind the 'Siegfried Line' they remained in their own positions; the British people would wait nervously for the coming war to unfold in earnest.

The men of the BEF had been arriving in some numbers since mid September 1939, when the first troops had stepped off the boat at Le Havre,

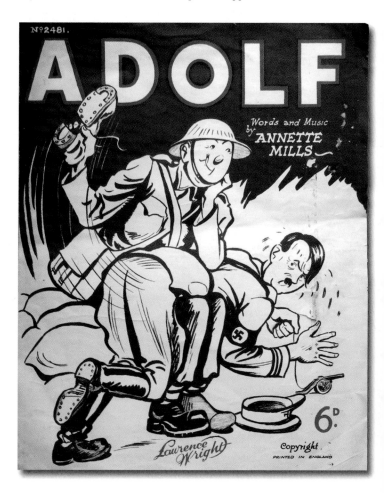

Adolf, a popular song from 1939, written by Annette Mills. The cover of the sheet music suggests that the British Army would be spanking the German Chancellor where it hurt.

just like their fathers before them. The British soldier of 1939–40 was in transition; the majority were untrained and untried conscripts and Territorials – the regular army forming little more than a cadre. Nevertheless, the BEF was confident in its abilities. In fact, the first test of British resolve in action was to be in the difficult conditions of Norway, when a misguided joint British–French venture was staged in April 1940 to attempt to deny Norway – with its North Sea-facing ports and huge natural resources – to the Germans. This experiment was to fail, and the resolve and confidence of the German forces were not to be seriously tested. In France and Belgium, the British hoped that the results would not be repeated.

When the German assault came in the early hours of the morning on 10 May 1940, it was swift and decisive. Piercing the French lines at Sedan and into the Ardennes, the Germans had hit hard at a weak point; for the fiercely proud French, determined to hold on at all costs to the long-contested soil of Alsace and Lorraine, the strongest positions of the Maginot Line were intended to protect them, with the best troops. The BEF took up its now traditional position in Flanders, alongside weaker French troops stationed opposite the Ardennes uplands. Defensive positions were much weaker here; the insistence of the Belgians that they were to remain neutral, come what may, disallowed the BEF and its French allies from placing themselves in a more favourable position within Belgium itself. The British would have to wait to be asked to move into Belgium, if threatened by its more belligerent neighbours.

The British plan of campaign – when attacked – was to take up a defensive position at the River Dyle (Plan D), one of the many rivers that crossed Flanders, with the option to retreat to successive river lines when attacked. On 10 May 1940, Operation *Sichelschnitt*, the German assault through the Ardennes, stove in the French lines at Sedan, cutting the Allies in half, and swept the Belgians aside farther north. With flanks in the air, the BEF had no choice but to retreat to the River Escaut, and then back to the frontier position as the Germans wheeled around to surround it. Despite a spirited counter-attack near Arras, and disciplined defence around the perimeter, Field Marshal Lord Gort knew that his time was running out and, ignoring ill-founded requests for further offensive action, took the decision to retreat to the coast with the aim of disembarking from the port of Dunkirk. With a defensive perimeter set up, Operation *Dynamo*, the rescue of the BEF from France, was put in place on 26 May. Picked up from the mole at Dunkirk by larger ships in the harbour itself, or wading out into the shallows from the beaches to the east of the port to be picked up by the 'little ships' – assorted craft whose role it was to ferry men to larger ships standing off the beaches – over 350,000 men were rescued, 150,000 of them French. The 'miracle of Dunkirk' was complete by 4 June 1940, but the last of the British Army in France would not leave, from Le Havre, until 14 June.

Left:
New recruits to the Royal Engineers, 1939.

Below:
One of the 'little ships' still stranded on the sands of Dunkirk. A flotilla of assorted craft like this did valuable work in May–June 1940 by ferrying men from the beaches to the waiting ships. Some, like this one, never made it back home.

In total 140,000 men would be left behind, most to spend the rest of the war as prisoners in camps across the Reich.

The return from Dunkirk was seen as a triumph by many, a relief that, at last, Britain was free from 'unreliable' allies. Faced with the withdrawal from Dunkirk, a withdrawal as famous as that from Gallipoli in 1915 (an event that saw Churchill fall from power as the First Lord of the Admiralty), the Prime Minister was defiant. With the German forces poised on the edge of mainland Europe to strike at England itself, Churchill was to deliver one of the most famous speeches in history: 'We shall fight them on the beaches, in the fields, and in the towns and cities, we shall never surrender.'

THE SOLDIER OF 1939–40
'Battledress' was to define the profile of the British soldier throughout the Second World War and well into the post-war period. Yet it was not widely available until 1939, and several units departed for France still wearing the uniform of their fathers. Battledress was an innovation based on the two-

piece ski-suits fashionable during the 1930s. It comprised a suit of khaki serge cut as a short jacket and voluminous high-waisted trousers. Battledress was worn with black 'ammunition' boots, a pair of heavy grade cotton webbing anklets replacing the puttees of the earlier generation.

The Field Service (FS) cap was the strange choice of headgear that replaced the peaked Service Dress cap with the introduction of battledress in 1939–40. Often called a 'side cap', it was worn perched on the right side of the head – the most fashion-conscious soldiers wearing it as far over on the right side as possible, a difficult proposition given the copious amounts of hair oil used. In action, the steel helmet replaced the FS cap. Its origins lay in the First World War, with its dish-like shape and broad rim suited to the trenches, providing protection from shrapnel falling from above. An improved version, the Mark II, was to appear in 1938. This was to see active service in all theatres, and would help define the distinctive profile of the British 'Tommy' in action.

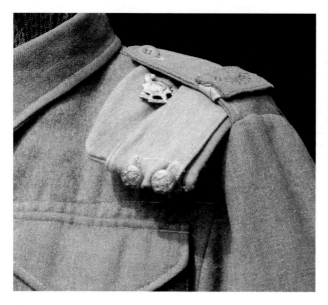

Above:
A battledress blouse and Field Service Cap for a soldier in the Royal Sussex Regiment. The FS cap was impractical to wear, but at least it tucked neatly beneath the shoulder straps.

Right:
A smartly turned-out recruit to the Royal Army Service Corps, pictured in battledress and Field Service Cap in 1939. Apart from his lanyard, the only distinction his battledress blouse has is a pair of drab slip-on shoulder titles with the initials of his Corps.

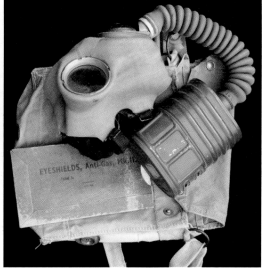

Above: Mark II infantry helmet complete with camouflage net. 'Cammo' nets were more common later in the war; early attempts to break up the distinctive silhouette of the 'Tommy' helmet used hessian or sacking covers similar to those employed in the First World War.

Above right: The Service respirator, an efficient but cumbersome anti-gas defence.

Right: The 1937 Pattern Webbing Equipment set, used throughout the war – with modifications – and beyond.

The British soldier was equipped with a pattern of webbing that was first introduced in 1937, developed in response to the advent of new weapons, such as the Bren light machine gun. The set was issued with pouches that could each carry fifty .303-calibre rifle bullets in five-round chargers, two curved Bren magazines, or hand grenades. No entrenching tool was considered at first, as it was thought that mechanised warfare had rendered it obsolete; this ideal was soon dispelled and a new tool added to the set.

The advent of gas warfare in the First World War was to influence tactical considerations in the inter-war period. The Small Box Respirator (SBR), developed in 1916, was an efficient means of counteracting most gases. The Service respirator that replaced it in 1926 was a development of the earlier version, but with a more substantial rubber face piece. The respirator was carried in a haversack with a strap that could be shortened to be worn high on the chest in the alert position. For those soldiers wearing spectacles, special flat-sided prescription glasses were issued that could be worn beneath the mask of the respirator itself. Each soldier was also equipped with comprehensive anti-gas over-clothing, designed to combat the variety of blister gases available. This set included capes, over-trousers and over-boots, as well as a hood to cover the helmet. The gas cape was carried in an alert position on top of the haversack; its widespread use declined as the war progressed.

The principal weapon of the British soldier from 1902 and well into the Second World War was the Short, Magazine, Lee Enfield rifle – SMLE,

Rack of typical examples of the Lee Enfield Rifle No. Mark III, workhorse of the British infantryman.

The universal or 'Bren Gun' Carrier, used in all theatres, here driven by Fusilier Victor Morris of the Royal Fusiliers, in 1941, who would see action overseas in Normandy (see page 60).

re-designated 'Rifle Number 1' in 1926. The Rifle No. 1, Mark III, introduced in January 1907, was a workhorse of the First World War; from January 1916, simplifications to this rifle were made in order to speed up production. The Rifle No. 1 Mark III* continued in service as the standard arm of the British soldier throughout the inter-war period, and was issued with a 17-inch-long 'sword' bayonet of Great War vintage. Although targeted for replacement in 1941, the Rifle No. 1 was never to be fully supplanted by its replacement, the Rifle No. 4, Mark I.

The Mark I Bren light machine gun, developed pre-war and still in service in some countries today. This one dates from 1942.

ONE MAN'S WAR: PRIVATE LESLIE DOYLE

Private Doyle was one of the many conscripts to the new Militia in 1939. Aged twenty in November, he was drafted into the newly formed army as Hitler was preparing his forces for the onslaught in the west. Joining the 5th Battalion King's Own Royal Regiment, he trained in Lancaster, and was shipped out to France with the rest of his battalion, forming a consitituent part of the Territorial 42nd (East Lancashire) Division. Like other raw troops, he visited the Maginot Line defences farther south, and experienced life in the front line so confidently expected to hold German territorial ambitions. Like other men of the BEF, he would write home about the mundanity of life in France, waiting for something to happen. Taking up position on the defensive lines to the north, in more

Private Leslie Doyle of the 5th King's Own Royal Regiment (bottom right) pictured with other men in Stalag VIIIB who were captured by the Germans during the retreat to Dunkirk.

hastily improvised positions dug by the BEF, he found himself on the right of the British line on the Escaut when the German assault broke on 10 May 1940. Attacked by Stuka dive-bombers, the French to the right of his company retired. They had no choice but to retreat in the ever-contracting perimeter to Dunkirk, forming part of the defensive rear-guard. Private Doyle would never make it to the sands of Dunkirk; he was captured at Hazebrouck on 1 June 1940, and was marched into five long years of captivity in Stalag VIIIB Lamsdorf, in Silesia.

The Bren light machine gun was first introduced to the British Army in 1937, and was used by British forces throughout the war, and in all theatres. Designed in 1935, it was actually based on a Czech design (the name Bren from a hybrid of the names of the Czech city of Brno and the Royal Small Arms Factory at Enfield), modified to take the standard rimmed .303 cartridge – the same ammunition as the Rifle No. 1. Gas-operated, the Bren was fed through a 30-round detachable curved box magazine, and had a rate of fire of around 500 rounds per minute, with an effective range of 600 yards. The Bren was carried in action by infantry sections, and lent its name, unofficially, to the handy tracked vehicles introduced during pre-war mechanisation – the 'Bren gun carrier' or 'universal carrier'. In action with the BEF, these would be left behind with all other vehicles during the retreat from Dunkirk.

HOME DEFENCE, 1940–4

A FTER DUNKIRK, with the remnants of the British Army safely back in Kent and Sussex, Winston Churchill had to remind his nation that wars were not won by retreats. Against a buoyant enemy, an enemy who had swept aside some of the strongest and best-equipped armies of western Europe, Britain was especially vulnerable. Home defence was a serious responsibility; the majority of the army would spend much of its war stationed at home, symbolically waving a fist at mainland Europe in the manner of David Low's famous cartoon of June 1940.

From 1939, defences were constructed to protect vulnerable areas and regions – anywhere where invasion from the sea could be a possibility. Yet, invasion was not entertained as a serious proposition until the onset of the German offensive in the west on 10 May 1940. From this point on, every address in Britain was to receive a copy of the terrifyingly frank leaflet 'If the Invader Comes'.

By the end of May 1940, under General Ironside, Commander-in-Chief Home Forces, the island was made into a fortress. The coast was made into a no-go area, with concrete fortifications, pillboxes, tank traps, barbed wire and gun emplacements forming fortified 'stop lines' intended to slow and break the momentum of Blitzkrieg. General Sir Alan Brooke replaced the rigid stop lines with 'defence-in-depth' in July 1940, breaking the lines into strong points backed up by the static defenders of the Home Guard, with fluid defence elsewhere – this was to remain in force for the rest of the war.

Traditionally, it was the Territorial Army that was to defend Britain's shores, and many of its infantry battalions had been retrained and refitted before the war as anti-aircraft units of the Royal Artillery. Controlled by Anti-Aircraft Command, there were in addition eight Home Commands, geographical entities each with a General Officer Commanding (GOC), who would be in charge of their defence and organisation. Anti-Aircraft (or 'Ack-Ack', after the signallers' phonetic spelling of 'AA') defences were to be gradually built up throughout the early part of the war, with the men, and later the women of the twelve divisions of Anti-Aircraft Command (under

Opposite:
Scots Guards
training with a Bren
gun in the UK.
(IWM HU 101296)

17

David Low's famous cartoon, from June 1940. The caption reads, 'Very well, alone!' and captures the spirit of the British people in the aftermath of Dunkirk.

General Frederick Pile) crewing the guns and searchlights. These divisions, part of the Air Defence Great Britain, were regionally distributed to afford maximum protection. On 10 September 1940 'every gun was to fire every possible round' into the sky with the opening of the London Barrage; this massed gunnery was to drive the Blitz attackers higher into the inky night sky. The responsibilities of AA Command never slackened during the war, and

AA Command insignia – they leave no doubt about the role of the units that wore them.

new methods were needed to try to shoot down flying bombs during the V-weapon offensives of 1944–5.

The Home Guard was born of an announcement made by Anthony Eden, the Minister for War, in 1940, at a time when the invasion of the UK seemed imminent. Raised as the Local Defence Volunteers (LDV) following a radio broadcast by the Secretary of State for War on 14 May 1940, in the first year of its existence the LDV was under-equipped and under-uniformed. Yet while the BEF faced disaster in France and Belgium, the LDV prepared sincerely to tackle one of the most formidable armies in history. Renamed the Home Guard in July 1940, at its height it was an army of around 1.7 million men. Its role was, at first, to watch out for paratroopers and seaborne raiders, and then to defend and hold static 'nodal' points long enough for the regular troops to attack. By 1943–4, the tide of the war had turned and a defensive force of the scale of the Home Guard was no longer sustainable, and it was stood down finally in September 1944.

The inadequacies of the army of 1939–40 highlighted the need for training. No longer would it be adequate to form an infantry division, as one observer was to comment, by 'tipping everything into a pot, and stirring well' with the hope that a finished product would appear from the concoction. For many infantry divisions, the majority of their war service would be spent at home, both defending vulnerable points on the mainland under the ultimate control of the Home Defence Commands, and training hard. The General Commanding 59th Division set out his strategy: 'We are training to produce a division which can act quickly to destroy or drive into the sea any Germans who have the temerity to come here; we are training to ensure steadfastness in battle; we must train all the time.' After Dunkirk, training took on a new urgency, and required realism in order to create battle hardening. From 1942, this training was focused on making soldiers 'offensively minded', and a large number of specialist schools were established up and down the country.

Late-war Home Guard uniform and equipment set. In June 1940, the fledgling Local Defence Volunteers would be equipped with little more than an armband and 'pike'.

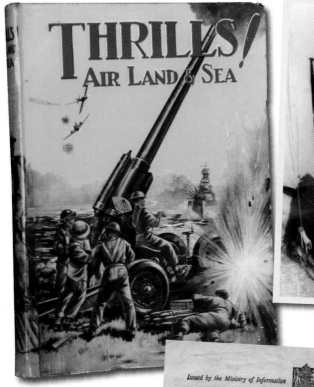

Above: A British 3.7-inch AA gun as depicted on a child's book cover, 1940.

Above right: Fusilier Thomas Stafford of the Northumberland Fusiliers, in training on Salisbury Plain, in full battle order. Fusilier Stafford would later see action in the Western Desert (see page 35).

Right: 'If the Invader Comes' – practical advice given by the Government and delivered to each door in 1940.

Wartime postcards extolling the virtues of British armour; however, many were too slow, under-gunned and under-armoured.

'The army hardens up'. This contemporary feature in *Picture Post* set the scene for the training needed by the British Army if it was to take the war back to Hitler.

Two tank brigades were committed to the BEF in 1940, and those men who returned did so without their armoured vehicles, abandoned in the Dunkirk perimeter and elsewhere. Expansion and rearmament were to follow: many tanks were obtained through the Lend-Lease arrangements with the United States, and homegrown versions were developed and produced by the energised workforce, much of it female. By the end of the war, the Royal Armoured Corps would have on its strength almost 22,000 tanks of all classes (light, cruiser and infantry), together with almost 10,000 armoured cars. They would lose almost 16,000 tanks in action.

New arms (such as the Reconnaissance Corps) and new services (such as the Royal Electrical and Mechanical Engineers) were to be developed in order to maximise the potential of the armoured strength of the British Army. The Reconnaissance Corps was raised in 1941, and was intended to be the eyes of the army, reconnoitring with armoured cars and armed

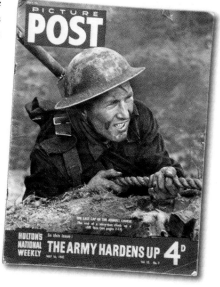

universal carriers in advance of an infantry division. Essential in a war of movement, its role was to determine the lie of the land and the disposition of enemy troops on the battlefront, and it was also able to engage the enemy where necessary.

The Royal Electrical and Mechanical Engineers, widely known as the REME, was a unit raised to fulfil a role that was of the greatest importance in mechanised warfare: the repair and upkeep of military vehicles. The REME was established in May 1942, the functions of vehicle repair and upkeep being transferred from two other services, the Royal Army Ordnance Corps (RAOC) and the Royal Army Service Corps (RASC). With vast numbers of vehicles left behind in France after Dunkirk, all services would have a job to do in restoring the mobility of the army. The REME was engaged wherever there were vehicles in action.

THE SOLDIER RE-EQUIPPED, 1941–4

The 200,000 British soldiers who returned from Dunkirk came home with limited arms and equipment, and their uniforms were worn and torn. Re-equipment was pressing and urgent – not just with the hardware, the trucks, armour and guns that were abandoned on the beaches of Flanders, but also with the provision of uniforms that would provide a unified image for the army as a whole. From late 1940 onwards, new weapons, new uniforms, new insignia, and new heavy equipment all started to appear as the nation geared itself for total war. Frills were dispensed with, and functionality was to be the watchword. A simplified or 'economy' version of the battledress was to appear in 1942 (often called the 1940 pattern) that was to be the work-a-day dress of the British soldier. Increasingly, though, these drab uniforms would come to be adorned by colourful insignia (shoulder titles, 'arm-of-service' strips, formation signs) that were intended both as unit identification, and as a means of developing *esprit de corps*.

In the same vein, the rakish but impractical Field Service cap would be replaced by the beret-like General Service cap, which although practical was awkward and incapable of being moulded to a stylish shape, unlike the wool berets of specialist arms such as the Royal Armoured Corps or the Airborne Divisions. And with brass and other metals valuable for the production of munitions, for the first time in their history the distinctive regimental cap badges of the British Army were made in plastic.

A new rifle and bayonet were also introduced. Although the No. 4 Mark I was first accepted into service in 1931, mass production was not to start until 1940. It was to be easier to manufacture: differing from the previous mark, it had a strengthened bolt action, a heavier barrel (notably protruding beyond the foresight), and a relocated back sight. The sword bayonet was replaced with a simple, 8-inch spike, known to most as the 'pig-sticker'.

Sleeve insignia from Fusilier Victor Morris (see page 60), while he served in the Royal Fusiliers, part of the junior brigade (denoted by the three infantry red arm-of-service strips) of the 80th Division. Such colourful insignia proliferated in 1941–2.

Simplified 'economy' battledress (often termed '1940 pattern', though first issued in 1942) with web equipment. This type of battledress dispensed with the fly front and concealed buttons of the earlier version, expensive design features.

The Rifle No. 1 Mark III*, trusted by the infantryman in two world wars (top), illustrated with its replacement (the rifle below), the Rifle No. 4 Mark 1, which was to see service in the North European Campaign.

Right: Plastic cap badges, introduced from 1942 as an economy measure to save on brass and other vital metals.

Below: General Service Caps, introduced to replace the less practical, but more raffish FS cap in 1942. An officer's quality version (bearing the red hackle of the Black Watch) and Other Ranks' version (from the Manchester Regiment) are illustrated.

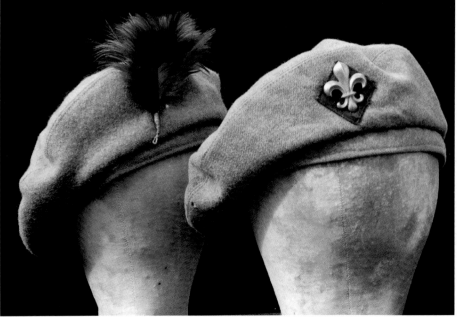

Mass production of the No. 4 rifle meant that the total British production reached two million by the war's end, with a further million or so supplied from North America.

New tanks, armoured vehicles and other materials of war would also be forthcoming from the United States under the Lend-Lease agreement brokered between Churchill and Roosevelt; from 1943, Britain would receive over $30 million of aid, with a quarter of munitions in British service being derived from this source.

ONE MAN'S WAR: LIEUTENANT C. R. JOHNSON

Lieutenant Johnson from Staffordshire joined the army as a volunteer in the early days of the war at the age of twenty-four. Joining a field artillery unit, he was to rise through the ranks to serve as a Lance-Sergeant as part of a 25-pounder field gun crew with the 61st Field Regiment, RA. Not deployed overseas in the early part of the war, Johnson was selected for officer training, and having completed his course of instruction he was transferred to Anti-Aircraft Command, serving at home with the 75th LAA Regiment. With a specialism in signals, Lieutenant Johnson liaised with the RAF, ensuring that AA Command reached its real target. Life lacked the frisson of excitement provided by field command, and revolved around liaison and mess bills. Eventually called overseas, he embarked for Alexandria and the Mediterranean theatre in 1942. He also saw service in northern Europe in 1944–5; requesting a transfer back to field command, he was to finish the war in action in Germany. Lieutenant Johnson would see for himself the collapse of Hitler's Reich.

The papers and personal effects of Lieutenant C. R. Johnson, Royal Artillery.

FROM THE DESERT
TO ITALY, 1940–5

THE LONG ROAD back to mainland Europe for the British soldier began through the sands of the Western Desert. After the many reverses of 1940–1, the defeats in France and Norway, the failure in Crete and mainland Greece, and even the logistics-driven, to and fro battles in Egypt, Libya and other territories on the African border of the Mediterranean, British and Commonwealth forces were to turn the tide at El Alamein. This pivotal battle, conducted by Lieutenant General (later Field Marshal) Bernard Law Montgomery was to change the course of the war, and turn the tide in the favour of the Allies in what Winston Churchill dubbed 'the end of the beginning' of the war.

The war in the desert commenced with Italian ambitions to expand its North African Empire beyond Libya to link with Italian East Africa. Declaring war on the Allies in June 1940, Italy opened its operations with small-scale raids against Egypt. The British answered with the same approach, and the first of many of Churchill's irregular 'bands of brigands and cut throats', the Long Range Desert Group (LRDG) was to see action. Many more, including the Special Air Service (SAS), would be formed in this way. The British forces in Egypt were there primarily to protect the Suez Canal, but included an armoured training division that was to grow into the 7th Armoured Division. Adopting a red jerboa as its formation sign, this force was to become known as the 'Desert Rats', although the soldiers themselves were content to call themselves the 'Mickey Mouse Division'. Nevertheless, they were to develop into a respected elite.

Overcommitted, poorly equipped and led, the Italian offensive of 9 September 1940 was soon halted – much to the ire of Mussolini – and three months later, the British counter-attacked. On 9 December, during Operation *Compass*, Tobruk was captured and the Italians were forced into a headlong retreat. Intercepting the Italians at Beda Fomm on 6 February, the 7th Armoured Division was to take 130,000 prisoners at a cost of 2,000 British and Commonwealth casualties. The abject failure of the Italians to progress their war alone was to force the reluctant Germans to bolster their

Opposite:
A Long Range Desert Group (LRDG) Dodge truck negotiating a sand dune in the desert, March 1941. The LRDG was to serve as the eyes of the army, carrying out long-range reconnaissance patrols.
(IWM E 2298)

Above:
The cloth insignia
of the 7th
Armoured Division,
the 'Desert Rats';
this is the second
pattern, adopted
later in the war.

Right:
British soldiers
at rest in Egypt,
showing the
variability of
uniform type.

weaker ally. From this point on the Afrikakorps Deutsches Afrikakorps (DAK) would be the dominant Axis force in the desert, and the reputation of its leader, Erwin Rommel, would be built.

Rommel launched two offensives penetrating deep into Egypt – offensives that continued the ebb and flow of the desert war. Rommel's first thrust in March 1941 recaptured the ground so easily relinquished by the Italians, and got close to the Egyptian border. The coastal town of Tobruk was besieged, and for much of the remainder of 1941 the British-led 8th Army (which included five Commonwealth nationalities together with Free French and Polish forces) attempted to break it. The exploits of this desert army were to capture the public imagination during difficult times. Operation *Crusader*, launched in November, pushed the German-led Axis forces back deep into Libya once again. Demands elsewhere meant that the experienced 7th Armoured Division was withdrawn, and in his second assault in January 1942 Rommel once more pushed the British back. In June, Rommel renewed his offensive, and following the armoured battle that

Left:
'Slip-on' covers for uniform shoulder straps, bearing the insignia of the 8th Army, a Crusader's shield. The cross was made yellow instead of red in order to avoid confusion with the red cross worn by stretcher bearers. Slip-ons were manufactured so that they could be removed for laundering.

Below:
Headlines from the *Daily Mirror* celebrating Monty's success at El Alamein.

became known as the 'Cauldron', Tobruk fell. Seemingly unstoppable, the Axis advance would finally be halted by the 8th Army, just seventy miles from Alexandria, in the First Battle of Alamein.

Dissatisfied with recent events, Winston Churchill replaced the British command with two new figures, General Harold Alexander as Commander-in-Chief of Middle East Command, and Lieutenant General Bernard Montgomery in charge of the 8th Army. Just as Rommel's appointment had galvanised the Axis forces, so this change at the top meant that the Allied desert forces would take on a new, dynamic role against the Axis. Quick to the offensive, Montgomery was to push back Rommel in August, but his most decisive move was the Second Battle of El Alamein in October–November 1942. After fighting in the Western Desert for three years, the British Army had turned a corner, and the long string of defeats at the hands of the Wehrmacht had finally been reversed. El Alamein also helped smash

the myth of German invincibility; from that point on, well armed, well led and confident, British forces would no longer feel technically inferior to their enemy – though it is to be doubted whether the average British Tommy ever felt *actually* inferior to the average 'Jerry'. In a battle that changed the course of the war, the Afrikakorps was forced into a retreat that spanned the width of Libya (with the fall of the capital, Tripoli), and entered Tunisia in February 1943. Rommel was recalled to Germany.

Four days after the victory at Alamein came Operation *Torch*, then the largest amphibious landing known, with 500 ships and over 100,000 American and British troops committed against Vichy French-held beaches in Morocco and Algeria. The landings in early November 1942, commanded by General Dwight D. Eisenhower, were a

Above: The Africa (left) and Italy (right) Stars, awarded with other campaign medals for service in the Mediterranean theatres. There were three clasps to the Africa Star: two of them denoted service in one of the two armies deployed (8th Army and 1st Army); the other, 'North Africa 1942–43', was for service in the 18th Army Group Headquarters, in the RAF, or in the Royal or Merchant Navy.

Right: Personal papers relating to the service of Second Lieutenant H. C. Watts, Royal Artillery, who was to fight his way through Italy, first landing in Sicily with the gunners. Montgomery's personal message thanking his troops for the success of the invasion of Sicily is amongst them.

Eighth Army

Personal Message from the Army Commander

To be read out to all Troops

campaign in SICILY is over. We landed in the island on ... together with our American allies, we had driven the ... th-east corner of the island.

I told you we would now drive the Germans out of SICILY ... ugust the Germans had been driven out, and the Allie ... ·n and British, were in possession of the whole island,

last the Italian overseas empire had ceased to exist ... 1943, we have captured our first slice of the Ital ...

events, you, the soldiers of the Eighth Army, ... part. By your splendid fighting qualities ... ·elped to change the whole course of the ... tell you my true feelings. Since ... ·· in August 1942, exactly one ... nd you have never failed

...THER, YOU AND I, WE ... E END.

B. L. MONTGOMERY
General
Eighth Army

success. Within weeks, the two Allied forces had converged at Tunis, and it was here, on 12 May 1943 that the Afrikakorps finally surrendered.

The way was open for the invasion of Italy, the Axis's weakest link, through Sicily. Operation *Husky*, the invasion of Sicily, opened the Italian campaign on 9–10 July 1943. The British, Canadian and American landings, using amphibious and airborne troops, were a success, although the Axis forces escaped to the mainland on 17 August 1943, abandoning the island to its fate. Assaulting the mainland of Italy, with its easily defended central rocky spine, was to be another matter.

The campaign in Italy was one of the most costly fought by the Allies, and was to be a point of disagreement between the British and Americans. Impatient to get the war against the Germans under way, the Americans favoured an invasion of Europe as soon as possible after the defeat of the Axis in Africa, with no diversions of effort or resources on 'sideshows'. Churchill felt otherwise; to him the 'soft underbelly of Europe' was a tantalising way of attacking the Reich by the back door. Roosevelt was also convinced that knocking Italy out of the war would more than repay the effort of invasion. Yet Italy was to prove to be no picnic. The men of the Italian campaign had cause to feel aggrieved, since they were largely forgotten when the assault on northern Europe opened in June 1944; nevertheless, they would wear their nickname of 'D-Day Dodgers' with ironic pride.

Above left:
British soldiers
in Italy.

Above:
British soldiers of
the 56th Infantry
Division in action
with a Bren gun at
Anzio, March 1944.
(IWM NA 13273)

The battle-hardened British 8th Army was to land on the toe of Italy on 3 September 1943 and proved too much for the Italians. An armistice with the invaders followed shortly afterwards on 8 September. The Germans, however, were in no mood to hand over Italy to their enemies so easily, and what followed was one of the most costly European campaigns of the Second World War. Further Allied landings, by the American-led 5th Army, took place on 9 September – the British at Taranto, and the Americans, heavily opposed, at Salerno. The Allies would battle their way up the peninsula, the British in the east, the Americans in the west, the port of Naples being the target. As the Allies battled northwards, the difficulty of the terrain became a major issue. The Germans had largely abandoned southern Italy as a dead loss; they were later to exploit and aggressively defend the terrain advantages given to them by the 3,000-foot Appennine Mountains farther north.

By October 1943 the Germans had laid out defensive lines that would serve to contain the Allies as far south – and therefore as far away from Germany – as possible. The most famous of these was the Gustav Line, which,

'Invasion Lire' and a guide book to Rome issued to the British Army in Italy.

together with other minor positions, proved to be a major obstacle at the end of 1943, halting the Allies in mountain snowstorms. The Gustav Line was to prove almost impregnable, and it took repeated offensives by the multi-national 8th and 5th Armies (with British, American, Canadian, French and Polish troops) to break it, between January and May 1944. One particular position, that of the mountain-top monastery of Monte Cassino, was to become infamous, a by-word for the strength of the positions, and the tenacity of its defenders. This was to prove one of the toughest nuts to crack, an essential objective in the invasion route of the Allied forces up the spine of the Italian peninsula. Four battles were fought between 24 January and 18 May 1944 for the control of Monte Cassino. Assaulted by Allied troops of many nations, the monastery was finally taken on 18 May 1944.

Rome fell to the US forces that were previously bottled-up at Anzio on 4 June 1944. The way ahead into northern Italy was blocked by another defensive position, the Gothic Line, along the Appennine mountain chain between Florence and Bologna. An offensive by the 8th and 5th armies on 25 August, Operation *Olive*, saw no decisive breakthrough, and the war ground to a halt, with little hope of resuming the attack in early 1945 owing to the severity of the winter weather conditions. The Allies were forced to sit and wait for spring. The final phase commenced on 9 April 1945, and by

Above left: Lance Corporal Norman Simpson, a dispatch rider with the RASC in Italy and the Western Desert, in aertex shirt and Khaki Drill trousers. Norman Simpson was shot through the cheek while pursuing his duties, but survived the war.

Above: 'War Aid' battledress of a Second Lieutenant in the Middlesex Regiment. These uniforms were manufactured in the USA and were issued to troops serving in Italy.

the end of that month the Axis forces were beaten; the Germans formally surrendered on 29 April, with the end of the war in Italy following on 2 May. Some 60,000 Allied soldiers had died, with total casualties reaching 320,000; for the Axis, this figure was over 658,000.

THE SOLDIER IN THE MEDITERRANEAN THEATRE, 1940–5

During the Great War, a lightweight uniform similar to the standard Service Dress and known as 'Khaki Drill' was worn in the warm climates of the Middle East, India and East Africa. This pattern of dress would be worn with shorts (one unloved, three-quarter-length pattern was dubbed 'Bombay bloomers') or trousers, and the archaic-looking Wolseley Pattern cork 'solar topee' intended to provide some respite from the searing sun. It would be worn at all tropical or warm-weather stations of Britain's shrinking colonial Empire well into the 1930s.

The men of the 8th Army, deployed in the Western Desert, adopted a style of dress that suited the informality of the desert conditions, and wore several species of Khaki Drill (KD) shorts, together with a new tropical shirt that was first issued in 1941. These long-sleeved pullover-type shirts were manufactured from an open-weave fabric known as 'aertex', worn commonly with slip-on loops bearing unit or formation insignia, such as the familiar 8th Army shield. From 1943, the open-necked 'bush shirt' made from KD or aertex was also introduced. Desert uniform style could be individual and idiosyncratic, typified by Jon's 'Two Types' (see illustration page 3), and General Montgomery himself.

Soldiers arriving in Italy lacked items of equipment, and particularly clothing, after their long engagement in the Western Desert. As such, they urgently required the issue of warmer clothing; this was provided from the United States as part of its Lend-Lease agreement, and is clearly marked, American style, as 'Battledress, Olive Drab, War Aid'. This was issued from 1943 onwards, and was unique in that it had the fly front of the first pattern battledress, while retaining the exposed buttons of the pockets. This type of battledress was to set apart those who had served in Italy from the rest of the army.

Soldiers in the typical uniform of the 8th Army, comprising shorts and aertex shirts.

ONE MAN'S WAR: FUSILIER THOMAS STANLEY STAFFORD

Fusilier Stafford was drafted into the Rifle Brigade in April 1940, and was to undergo training on Salisbury Plain during the dark days of 1940, when the nation was convinced invasion was imminent. On completion of training, Tom Stafford was transferred into the 4th Northumberland Fusiliers in December 1940, which embarked for the Middle East theatre. Equipped with universal carriers, Tom's unit took part in the war of movement in the desert – 'up the blue' with his mates. His battalion was transferred to reconnaissance duties in 1941; as a driver, Fusilier Stafford observed the dispositions of Axis troops as Rommel's offensives started to bite. In this swift-moving war, Tom Stafford and his comrades were overrun by the Germans in June 1942, and were taken prisoner by the Italians, later being transferred as prisoners of war to Germany, after the collapse of the Italians and the signing of their armistice. Like all other non-officer prisoners, he would be required to work in *Arbeitskommandos* throughout the Reich. After the long march westwards, Fusilier Stafford returned home in May 1945.

Above: Fusilier Tom Stafford (left) pictured with a friend in Egypt.

Left: Fusilier Tom Stafford with his Bren gun carrier; note his Wolseley Pattern 'solar topee', bearing the puggaree flash 'V' (denoting the Northumberland Fusiliers).

THE FAR EAST, 1940–5

B RITAIN maintained considerable overseas territories in the 1930s, part of a colonial Empire that had been built through centuries of British maritime influence. India was the jewel in the crown of the Empire; its vast territory and untapped resources were the envy of all colonial powers, not least of Japan, which from the early 1930s had harboured intentions to expand its sphere of influence away from its cramped islands. In 1937, Japan had invaded mainland China, and was engaged in a fierce war with the Chinese that was the result of centuries of rivalry in the region. With the attack on Pearl Harbor on 7 December 1941, severely depleting US naval strength, the Japanese intended to knock the Americans out of the action, and their sights were set on the Philippines, and on the Far Eastern territories of Britain and the other European powers, including the Dutch East Indies.

The British colony of Hong Kong, a territory of 410 square miles that had been leased to Britain in 1898, was attacked the day after the naval and aerial assault on Pearl Harbor. The garrison comprised 12,000 men – mostly from the Indian Army, but with British and Canadian battalions. Attacked with overwhelming force by the Japanese, the Allies retreated to within the island city itself, and although a spirited defence was made, the British forces stationed there were forced to surrender on Christmas Day, 1941. These men, like so many others, would be forced into a terrible captivity that was to be typical of the treatment of the Allied prisoners of the Emperor.

Malaya was also attacked on 8 December 1941. A vital target – Malaya supplied over 50 per cent of the world's rubber – the peninsula was a federation of states, with the British-controlled colony that comprised Singapore at its tip. The advance along the peninsula was rapid, the Japanese making use of the roads cut for the rubber workers, deploying men on bicycles and making use of light tanks. Singapore was defended by mostly Indian troops with a leavening of Australian, British and Malay units (seventeen Australian, thirteen British and two Malay battalions) that composed the 88,000-strong force. The newly arrived British 18th Infantry Division lacked experience and appropriate training; most of the other units

Opposite:
British soldiers
(Chindits) in
action with
a mortar during
operations
in Burma.
(IWM SE 7926)

Right: 'The Gang', 1941. In receipt of new tropical uniforms, these men may well have been on their way to Singapore; many would not return.

Middle left: Lieutenant General Sir Arthur Percival, who led and later surrendered the British defenders of Singapore to the Japanese in February 1942.

Middle right: The 15-inch guns at Singapore in action. It is often suggested they could not fire inland, which is inaccurate. They did, however, suffer from a shortage of high explosive (rather than armour-piercing) ammunition.

Left: Indian troops arriving in Singapore. Many remained loyal as prisoners of war, despite inducements from the Japanese to join the 'Indian National Army' to fight against the British.

were under strength. The fortress of Singapore was equipped with 15-inch large-calibre coastal guns; as coastal guns focused on firing on ships to the south, these were said to have been useless against a land force attacking from the north. (In fact, they were used against the Japanese, but were ineffective owing to their lack of high explosive shells.)

Led by Lieutenant General Sir Arthur Percival, the Allied force was relatively poorly equipped and certainly poorly trained – little match for (and out-generalled by) Lieutenant General Yamashita and his Japanese 25th Army, 30,000 veterans battle-hardened from the war in China. The attack on Singapore itself commenced on 7 February 1942. The colony would fall just eight days later, the Japanese penetrating the Allied lines through gaps formed by creeks and swamps, ultimately causing the Allied forces to contract inwards. Winston Churchill, believing the Japanese to be outnumbered, demanded no surrender from Percival on 10 February. Three days later, with the Allies still losing ground, senior officers advised Percival to surrender in an attempt to minimise civilian casualties. At first he refused, but faced with fierce attacks and decreasing supplies, he ruled out the possibility of a counter-attack. Unconditional surrender followed on 15 February, notorious as the largest surrender of British-led military forces in history – 80,000 Indian, Australian and British troops would be condemned to the hell of Japanese prison camps.

The British and Australian soldiers taken prisoner were incarcerated in Changi Prison, suffering hardships, sickness and casual deaths that would be

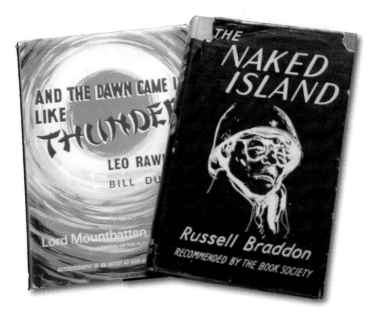

The inhuman conditions endured at the hands of the Japanese by Allied prisoners of war in the Far East are notorious, and have been the subject of many books.

common to all prisoners of war held by the Japanese. Thousands would be shipped on 'hell ships' across Asia, including Japan; those that survived would be used as forced labour on engineering projects such as the Burma–Siam Railway, and the Sandakan Airfield in Borneo. Although some Indian troops captured would join the Japanese against the British as part of the 'Indian National Army', others would stalwartly remain as prisoners alongside their comrades.

Formation sign for General 'Bill' Slim's 14th Army in Burma.

In January 1942 the Japanese continued their assault against British territories with the invasion of Burma, a large country with a challenging terrain that bordered India to the west, and China and hostile Siam to the north and east. The Japanese objectives in Burma were the capture of the capital Rangoon and the closure of the overland supply line to China, strengthening and defending Japanese gains in Malaya and the Dutch East Indies. Natural obstacles to this invasion were the major rivers that crossed Burma from south to north, the Irrawaddy, the Chindwin, the Sittang and the Salween. In addition, the tropical monsoon between May and October was to transform the already wet terrain into a quagmire.

The Japanese advance met weak opposition from under-strength British-led troops on the Burmese frontier: two regular British battalions, two Indian Army infantry brigades and local Burmese forces. As the advance gained momentum, Rangoon and Mandalay were to fall and the British forces withdrew to India, crossing the mountains at Imphal in May 1942. The difficulties of the terrain – particularly the impassability of the roads – together with pernicious disease took their toll on the retreating forces. As the British strategy shifted to the defensive, only limited

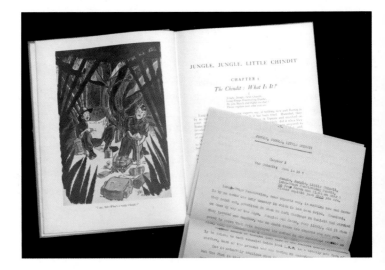

Jungle, Jungle, Little Chindit, published in 1945, takes a humorous view of the activities of Orde Wingate's famous Long Range Penetration forces in Burma.

offensives could be planned, and a widespread belief developed that the Japanese were almost superhuman jungle fighters. Operations in Burma in 1942–3 were hampered by the resource limitations of multi-front war; the Middle East, which was closer to home and involved fighting the Germans, was given priority in accordance with the 'Germany First' agreement between Britain and the USA. A limited offensive to recapture the Arakan coastal region was attempted in September 1942; against a strong defence this phase was to stagger to a close early in 1943.

The most celebrated component of the British offensive activities in Burma was the creation of the Chindits, the brainchild of the maverick Brigadier Orde Wingate, who believed in the development of 'Long Range Penetration' (LRP) to harry the Japanese lines. The name 'Chindit' was derived from a traditional Burmese temple guardian, the *Chinthe*, and was appropriate as the force was to operate within the Chindwin River area. The first Chindit operation, *Longcloth*, was carried out in February 1943, with some 3,000 men entering Burma to harry Japanese communications and supply lines. The operation was marred by high casualties, yet it demonstrated that British troops could fight on equal terms with the Japanese 'jungle superman'. In August 1943, South East Asia Command (SEAC) was created under Admiral Louis Mountbatten, and the British and Indian forces were united as the 14th Army under Lieutenant General William ('Bill') Slim. Slim was a charismatic general who had been promoted from the ranks in the First World War, and he was instrumental in improving the training, equipment, health and morale of his men to tackle the Japanese. Like the 8th Army in Italy, the achievements of the 14th Army were overshadowed by the activities in northern Europe; the Far East soldiers would come to believe they belonged to a 'forgotten army'.

In March 1944 the Japanese Army launched Operation *U-Go*, an attack on India intended to seize British supplies in Assam, inspire a rising by the Indian people against British rule and relieve pressure on other fronts in the Western Pacific. As with their 1942 campaign, the Japanese relied on mobility, infiltration and captured supplies to maintain the momentum of the attack. As the Japanese attacked northwards in the Arakan, British forces employed defensive boxes, supplied by air, to hold out against

British and Indian troops in action at Imphal in 1944.

Above left: The Burma Star and other campaign medals awarded to Private Grayling of the King's Royal Rifle Corps, for his service in the Far East.

Above right: The impeccably turned-out Sergeant A. Barker, serving in the Far East early in the war, with shirt, shorts and solar topee.

determined assaults until the Japanese were forced to withdraw, short of supplies. These tactics were again employed on a larger scale when Imphal and Kohima were surrounded.

The Japanese 15th Army consisted of three infantry divisions and a unit of the 'Indian National Army'. The Japanese commander planned to cut off and destroy the forward Allied forces, before capturing strategically important Imphal, on the main route to India, isolating the town by the capture of Kohima. These aims were not achieved; the defenders of Kohima were besieged for almost two weeks on 5–18 April before being relieved by the British 2nd Division, which began its own counter-offensive on 15 May. The fighting continued until the Japanese withdrew with heavy casualties, and the Imphal operation was finally abandoned in July. The Japanese retreated to the Chindwin River. This was the largest defeat they had suffered up to that point, with 55,000 casualties, including 13,500 dead – and with them, the reputation of the Japanese soldier as invincible. And while Japanese forces were fully engaged at Imphal and Kohima, a second Chindit expedition, *Thursday*, was launched. Establishing airfields and strongholds behind Japanese lines, Chindit columns harassed the Japanese and their supply lines. The operation was, however, marred by the death of Orde Wingate in an air crash.

Despite the onset of the monsoon in May 1944, General Slim's 14th Army continued to advance against the retreating Japanese towards the Chindwin River. By the end of 1944, the Allies were ready to advance onto the central plains of Burma. Using a combination of tanks and infantry, long columns, supplied by air, advanced southwards destroying the Japanese resistance. Amphibious landings started to take place on the Arakan coast and bridgeheads were established over the Chindwin and Irrawaddy rivers. Mandalay was captured on 20 March 1945; two months later Rangoon fell with the Japanese troops retreating to the River Sittang. The war in Burma had been won.

ONE MAN'S WAR: SECOND LIEUTENANT DONALD FLETCHER

Donald Fletcher had an unusual war, reflecting the complexities of the Far East theatre. He was one of very few men who were trained to fight the Japanese through the use of intelligence techniques. Studying for a Classics degree at Cambridge, he was plucked from academia after his first year of study in 1943, and enrolled on an officer-training course. Given his background, he was commissioned as a Second Lieutenant in the Intelligence Corps, sent to an outpost of the top-secret intelligence centre Station X in De Parys Avenue, Bedford. Here, in an intense academic hothouse, he would learn the rudiments of Japanese and the use of Japanese codes and ciphers, work essential in furthering the war in the Far East. Top secret for years, this work has been overshadowed in the post-war mythology of the activities of Bletchley Park in penetrating the German intelligence network. As part of the intelligence network, he was posted closer to the action in Darwin, Australia, and felt compelled to wear flashes bearing the words 'Great Britain' on his shoulder straps. Working on Japanese coded messages, he was the first to decipher the Emperor's surrender message to the Japanese forces in the Far East. Symbolically taking the salute at the surrender of a Japanese unit following the recapture of Singapore, he was to feel awkward and very English in the face of the pomp and gravity accorded to the surrender of one officer's Samurai sword in 1945, a souvenir that he brought back with him on his return to the UK. Donald Fletcher returned to Cambridge after the war.

Above left: (top) Typical felt slouch hat preferred by Chindits and other British forces serving in Burma. (Bottom) Wolseley Pattern overseas Service Helmet, or solar topee, issued as part of the early war tropical kit.

Above right: 1944 Pattern Jungle Green Webbing, developed in response to the needs of jungle warfare. Developed from the 1937 pattern set, it arrived too late to see much use in the Second World War.

Left: Pre-war Khaki Drill tunic of the type issued to highland troops, with the later issue 'Bush jacket' behind. Conspicuous Khaki Drill was less well suited to jungle warfare than the later issues of rot-proofed 'jungle greens'.

THE BRITISH SOLDIER IN THE FAR EAST, 1940–5

The Far East soldier was traditionally equipped at the opening of the Second World War. Those men stationed at the outposts of Empire in Hong Kong, Rangoon and Singapore wore the Khaki Drill and solar topee that had characterised the British soldier in tropical climes since the nineteenth century. This was the uniform worn by the defenders of Hong Kong and Singapore against the Japanese in 1941–2, equipped with steel helmet and Rifle No. 1. A heavy machete to cut back the cloying jungle was the only concession to locality.

Yet jungle fighting required more from uniforms and equipment than serving in more temperate or less humid climes. The heavy cotton or wool serge uniforms used in other theatres were hopelessly inadequate, as neither would keep the wearer cool in the humid, tropical heat. An open-weave fabric was required, as was appropriate headgear and cotton web equipment that would not rot under jungle conditions. New uniform items started to appear with the continuing war in Burma. Here, 'jungle green' uniforms made from treated rot-resistant open-weave aertex were made and issued, often supplied from India. Surviving examples are rare today. The Australian-style slouch hat was also worn; this could be mistreated, shaped to the wearer's own satisfaction, and was effective at keeping off the unrelenting sun. Later, bush hats similar to those still in use by most forces today were to be developed. American-style gaiters and special jungle boots were also designed to combat the heavy vegetation, and biting venomous insects, of the Burmese jungle.

Finally, the 1937 webbing equipment set, used in all theatres, was also to be given close scrutiny, given its propensity to rot in the unsavoury tropical, humid climate. A new equipment set, designated the '1944 Pattern', was designed for jungle use. Issued in rot-proofed 'jungle green' cotton web, it had redesigned haversacks, larger water bottles and the ability to suspend items of the American equipment, supplied with wire hooks, from its belt. This set, together with an improved helmet (the Mark IV) and cut down rifle (Rifle No. 5, the 'Jungle Carbine'), were available to the British at the end of the war, but would see most action after its close, in the post-war struggles in the last outposts of Britain's fading Empire.

British soldier in slouch hat and jungle clothing, Burma, 1945.

'DESERVE VICTORY', 1944–5

I N NORTHERN EUROPE, on both sides of the English Channel, there were preparations for the inevitable invasion – the 'Second Front', much called for by Communist activists in Britain after the Soviet Union was attacked by Hitler in 1943. From Spain to Norway, Hitler put much faith in – and expended much energy and resources on – the construction of his Atlantic Wall, itself intended to dissuade the Allies from invasion. Churchill would demand innovative ways of taking the fight back to mainland Europe.

The idea of the Commandos, a body of specially trained and well-equipped men (named after the tenacious Boer forces the Prime Minister had himself fought against forty years before) that could tackle the Nazis in their strongholds, was born in the dark days of June 1940, following the evacuation from Dunkirk and the delivery of Churchill's historic 'fight them on the beaches' speech on the 4th. The idea was received with enthusiasm by the Prime Minister, who had seen at first hand what could be achieved by these groups, and these men were the first regular forces to take the war back to Europe. The Army was first to raise its Commandos, building on the experience of the Independent Companies raised in April 1940 in order to harass, guerrilla-fashion, the Germans deployed in Norway. The Royal Marines followed suit in 1942, raising separate Royal Marine Commandos.

All Commandos were trained in amphibious operations, landing in secrecy, and engaging in offensive operations on a hostile shore. Volunteers had to have the physical attributes of an athlete, endurance, and the capability to kill without hesitation. Training was hard, and carried out in the difficult terrain of the Scottish Highlands at the specialist training centre set up at Achnacarry. In all, around thirty Commandos, highly mobile and self-contained units of Commando soldiers, were raised, twelve of them from the Army. Nine were raised from the Royal Marines, and No. 10 (Inter-Allied) Commando was composed of men from all the occupied Allied Nations. Ultimately successful, the Commandos were to attract the personal ire of Hitler himself, who issued his notorious *Kommandobefehl* in 1942 – no quarter was to be given to this new and deadly enemy if captured, even when

Opposite:
Men of the 15th
(Scottish) Division
crossing the Rhine
by assault craft,
24 March 1945.
(IWM BU 2154)

Above left: *Britain's Modern Army,* a contemporary book outlining the nature of the forces about to re-invade northern Europe. The book probably tied in with an exhibition about the army held on the site of the bombed John Lewis department store in London's Oxford Street.

Above right: Contemporary newspaper account of the disastrous Dieppe raid in 1942, with its headlines masking the Allied losses. Nevertheless, valuable lessons were learned for D-Day.

in uniform. Many were to be executed in concentration camps, in direct contravention of the Articles of the Geneva Convention.

The greatest raid of them all – at Dieppe in 1942 – was intended, it was said, to test German resolve and examine the possibilities of a large force taking and holding the perimeter of a major port. A 'raid in force' directed against the Normandy port, it was an abject failure with 4,131 men, mostly Canadians, left behind dead, wounded or captured, the new Churchill tanks being contained on the beach by the sea wall. The object of the raid has been a point of discussion and argument ever since those few men that could be were rescued from the beaches on 19 August 1942; but at the very least, its failure put into sharp focus the need for careful planning and specialist equipment – lessons that would be surely learned in time for the invasion of Normandy in 1944. British Commandos were deployed to secure the flanks, as they would be in 1944, and this they did successfully. Royal Marine Commandos were also to perform this significant role on D-Day: they secured the flanks of each separate beach area, ensuring that the forces that landed on them linked up, and taking troublesome strong points and minor garrisons in the process.

Born from the Commando idea was the creation of the Parachute Regiment; the use in combat of German *Fallschirmjäger* ('paratroopers') in capturing Fort Eben Emaul in 1940 and in the attack on Crete had demonstrated the importance of this new type of infantry. British paratroops were developed in late 1940, while the Parachute Regiment itself was formed in August 1942, composed eventually of eighteen battalions. Raised from No. 2 Commando, who had received parachute training, it was instilled in the paratroopers from early on in their training that they were an elite. Together with specially designated glider-borne infantry battalions and representatives of the arms and services, the men of the Parachute Regiment formed two airborne divisions, the 1st and the 6th. Both divisions could be distinguished by a formation sign, the claret and blue Pegasus badge, and all trained personnel of the airborne divisions wore the red beret that has become the distinctive insignia of the British airborne.

'Bellerophon astride Pegasus' – the classical theme used as the distinctive insignia of all British airborne troops.

British paratroops were deployed in Europe at the Bruneval raid of early 1942, and in Italy; but they would receive fame from their participation in Normandy, when the 6th Airborne secured the left flank of the invasion by capturing the bridges over the Orne ('Pegasus Bridge') and the Dives, and in Operation *Market Garden*, when the 1st Airborne held the 'bridge too far' over the Rhine at Arnhem. Operation *Market Garden* of September 1944 was one of the most audacious gambles of the war. The airborne assault was to take and hold the succession of bridges across waterways standing in the way of the Allies

Below: Commando cap badges: badge of the Army's No. 2 Commando (left); badge worn by all Royal Marine Commandos (right). The Green Beret, issued from 1943, would be worn by all.

Right: Sergeant James Evans of the 2nd Independent Parachute Brigade. Wounded in April 1944 at Monte Cassino, he was unable to participate with his comrades in the landings of the 1st Airborne Division at Arnhem in September.

Above:
British paratroopers check their equipment before emplaning during Operation *Market Garden*, September 1944. (IWM K 7591)

Above right:
Formation signs worn by the 21st Army Group Headquarters staff (top), and those of the 2nd Army (bottom).

who were slogging towards the Rhine and into Germany. In true airborne fashion, these troops were vulnerable behind the lines, fighting as self-contained units surrounded by the enemy. The relief would be by a mobile armoured column, supplied by the men of XXX Corps along a single road. As is well known, the final bridge over the Neder Rijn at Arnhem (taken intact by the men of the 1st Airborne) proved to be a 'bridge too far' for the XXX Corps, with the single 'Devil's Highway' proving too much of a logistical nightmare for rapid transit. The bridges were all captured intact, but with an unexpected concentration of enemy troops near Arnhem, and the difficulties of the route, the men of the 1st Airborne would take severe casualties, and many would join much earlier captives in prisoner-of-war camps. Arnhem was not retaken until much later in the war.

The opening of a 'Second Front' – fighting in the west to relieve the onslaught on the Soviet Union – had been the focus of attention for Communist activists in Britain since the USSR had been attacked in 1941. If nothing else, the abortive 'raid' at Dieppe in 1942 had confirmed the difficulty of attacking a well-defended shore from the sea. Any real invasion would take levels of planning, men, munitions and armour that would be beyond the Allies in 1942–3, but following the build-up of Allied forces in Britain, would become a reality. With America committed to the 'Germany First' policy over the Japanese, US troops arrived en masse in Britain, to be stationed the length and breadth of the island. From 1942 onwards, the extent of the build-up of forces in Britain was such that the island was to become both a huge troop ship and aircraft carrier alike. Although relations were usually cordial, there were some misunderstandings, British troops famously resenting the abundant pay and flashy uniform of the average GI.

Of the British divisions available to assault Europe, only a few had actually seen service overseas; the rest, fully equipped and raring to go, had been involved in training exercises designed to prepare and battle-harden the new recruits for an eventual return to northern Europe. This had been part of the British soldier's life since after Dunkirk, with most divisions stationed at home, while others were fighting in the Middle East and Far East theatres. There was a need to keep the army on its toes. Large-scale training exercises, drill with weapons and fitness with new weaponry were to be all-important and would finally pay off on D-Day, 6 June 1944, when they formed part of the British and Commonwealth military that landed as part of Montgomery's 21st Army Group. These were the men who would advance through northern Europe to the surrender of the German forces.

General Eisenhower was the popular choice for Commander-in-Chief of the Invasion Force. He was an able diplomat and leader, well liked and respected by all. Unafraid of taking decisions, Eisenhower also knew how to handle his men, and, particularly, the big personalities of the generals immediately under his command, such as Bernard Montgomery. Monty, triumphant leader of the 8th Army in the Western Desert and in Italy, was called to take charge of the Army Group that was actually to invade Europe in 1944. The 21st Army Group consisted of two armies, the 2nd British (Dempsey) and the 1st US (Bradley). British drive and ingenuity would be severely tested in the assault on fortress Europe.

Hitler's Atlantic Wall, Normandy. The Longues sur Mer battery would be taken intact by British troops on 6 June 1944.

The invasion beaches selected in 1943 were in Normandy; these provided sufficient tactical space for manoeuvre, and the Atlantic Wall defences – Hitler's very own Maginot Line designed to keep the western Allies at bay while he took on the might of the Soviet Union – were much weaker than those across the Straits of Dover in the Pas de Calais, just 22 miles away. The Normandy beaches were much farther away from the coast of Britain, but the Allies were not going to land in ignorance. Intelligence-gathering had been part of the Commandos' brief, with small-scale operations ascertaining, for example, whether the beach sands would support armour, and the scale of the defences recently bolstered by Montgomery's old adversary, General Erwin Rommel.

The Allies had comprehensive dossiers on all aspects of the chosen beaches, spreading from the River Douvres in the west, to the Orne and the Caen Canal in the east. The ground varied considerably: the British and Canadian landing beaches (code-named Gold, Juno and Sword), and one of the American beaches (Utah), were characterised by open shores backed by dune fields or sea walls. The remaining American beach (Omaha) was backed by cliffs. All would be difficult to invade, as Rommel had ensured that the beach defences were in good order, intended to stop an invader in a maze of so-called tetrads and 'Belgian hedgehogs', concrete and metal defences designed to rip the bottom out of thin-skinned invasion craft.

'Invaders Thrusting Inland' – the *Daily Mirror* reports the D-Day landings.

Instrumental in the success on the British and Canadian beaches against these defences was the 79th Armoured Division, led by Major General Hobart. Hobart was the originator of the 'funnies', a series of specialist armoured vehicles based on Sherman and Churchill tanks that were designed to take on the might of Hitler's Atlantic Wall fortifications. Examples included the 'crab' or 'flail' tank, intended to take out the minefields, and the AVRE (Armoured Vehicle Royal Engineers), which, equipped with a petard-firing weapon, could dispatch most concrete fortifications it met.

The first forces in action on D-Day were British; glider-borne troops of the 6th Airborne were tasked with the capture of the bridges across the Orne and Caen Canal at

Sherman 'flail' tank of the 79th Armoured Division, the flail being used to explode landmines. One of Hobart's 'funnies', tanks like these would be used to great effect on D-Day.

Caen was a tough nut to crack. The higher ground to the south and east of the city was strongly held by panzer troops. The 43rd Wessex Division was used to try to break the deadlock at Hill 112 in July 1944. These items belonged to Normandy Veteran Pte Victor Morris (page 60).

the eastern extremity of the 60-mile-long stretch of the invasion beaches. In an audacious move, the gliders landed adjacent to the Bénouville Bridge over the canal at 12.16 a.m. and captured it intact, denying this to German forces and securing the Normandy beaches. Renamed 'Pegasus Bridge' in honour of its captors, it is preserved with its bullet scars today.

The British and Canadian landings took place at around 7.30 a.m., after the Americans had come ashore at Utah and Omaha. Embarking from a range of specialist landing craft, they were everywhere opposed by the defenders. Resistance was, nevertheless, patchy on all beaches – toughest at the easiest beach to defend, Omaha, but tough elsewhere, too. The availability of specialist tanks from the 79th Armoured Division, reducing the defences and assaulting the defenders, was of the greatest significance. The 'funnies' had done their job well. By nightfall, the Allies had established their beach head and had captured the city of Bayeux, symbolic as the seat of the Duke of Normandy, William the Conqueror. Taking control of Caen, however, was to prove a much more difficult task.

British soldiers
advance cautiously
through a battle-
scarred north
German town,
1945.

The distinctive
black boar
formation sign
of XXX Corps.

Caen was the D-Day objective for the British 2nd Army, but its defenders
would not relinquish it so easily. The city was intended to be the pivot for the
Allied armies, swinging south and eastwards and assaulting the German
forces on a wide front. Without Caen there would be no easy way forward.
The toughest German panzer forces were concentrated on the high ground
to the south and east of the city; Omar Bradley and his 1st US Army slugged
it out in the hedgerow country known as the *bocage*. Montgomery committed
the British and Canadian troops to a string of battles in July 1944, including
operations *Charnwood* and *Goodwood*, to try to dislodge the Germans from
their vantage points, and move through into open territory. Tensions grew
between the Allies as the hold-up continued. Finally, in early August,
Canadian troops operating east of the city managed to force the Germans
back, and paved the way for the Allies to advance out of Normandy. Falaise
was to be the next target; here a gap in the lines between British and
American troops allowed some of the Germans to escape; the rest would be
destroyed by ground attack Typhoon aircraft of the RAF. By the end of
August, Paris had been liberated, and the way forward deep into Reich
territory was clear.

For the British, that advance would take them through France and once more into Flanders and the Low Countries, before reaching the Rhine. This included the ill-fated Operation *Market Garden* in September. The 'Club Route', a continuous advance by the British XXX Corps, plotted a hard-fought battle against tenacious and often fanatical defenders, matching the drive of the American forces farther south.

From their arrival in occupied Europe, British and Commonwealth soldiers were welcomed with open arms, often being treated like stars, and being entreated to supply kisses, handshakes and autographs. In some cases this impeded the advance of the army, as the crush of the grateful population of towns and cities in France and the Low Countries was effective in stopping armoured columns.

After his long campaign in northern Europe, the final honour of receiving the surrender of all German forces fell to Field Marshal Montgomery on 4 May 1945 at Lüneberg Heath; the final surrender of Germany was to follow three days later at General Eisenhower's headquarters in Rheims. When Victory in Europe (VE) Day, 8 May 1945, was finally announced by the BBC, it was late in the day, and the celebrations on that public holiday were impromptu and spontaneous.

"I feel just like a Film Star."

Advancing through northern France and the Low Countries, the British Liberation Army received a hero's welcome.

With victory came the hope that the armed forces would be quickly demobilised. The fact that the nation was still at war with the Japanese (VJ Day would not be for another two months) did not escape the average soldier. Wishing to get home as soon as possible, but expecting to be sent to the Far East, the average soldier would have to wait until 1946 before he was released from the clutches of the army. At this point, each soldier would be issued with his residual pay and allowances, and would trade in his uniform for a civilian suit or jacket and trousers – clothing being strictly rationed. This suit would enter mythology as the 'demob suit'. It was not until 8 June 1946 that a major celebration of the achievement of Britain and its Commonwealth was celebrated with a spectacular parade through the centre of London, a symbolic occasion of the remembrance of Britain's fortitude in the face of adversity, yet demobilisation would not be complete until 1947.

The France and Germany Star and other campaign medals awarded to Fusilier J. H. Jones of the Royal Welch Fusiliers, for service in the North West European campaign, 1944–5.

THE MEN OF 1944–5

Famously, 4911986 Fusilier Tom Payne of the 6th Royal Welch Fusiliers was pictured in France in June 1944 in battle order; the contents of his kit were illustrated for all to see, for the public to experience what it was like to carry his equipment into battle. In addition to his Mark III helmet, a Rifle No. 4, and a Verey pistol, he was wearing the standard 1940 pattern battledress in serge and 1937 pattern webbing equipment, together with a General Service (GS) spade – a more realistic prospect when it came to field fortifications. Every pack and piece of webbing was stuffed with useful items. First issued in 1943, the Mark III infantry helmet would be worn in action by some of the assault battalions at D-Day. It retained the Mark II liner of the earlier helmet, and the simple, elasticated Mark III chin strap of its predecessor, but was distinguished by its dished shape that provided much more protection for the back and sides of the head.

With the decrease in fears over the use of gas, a new compact respirator with integral filter unit was issued in 1941. This was contained in a green waterproof canvas pouch that could be either slung over the shoulder or strapped to the belt by means of brass hooks. As each respirator was fitted to individual requirements, it was essential that this be marked to its individual owner, as before; a new innovation was the issue of an additional red circular identity disc to be attached to the respirator case.

The uniform of the Commando was undistinguished, and largely devoid – in the early days at least – of distinguishing marks and distinctive

Above left:
In this famous picture, Fusilier Tom Payne of the 6th Royal Welch Fusiliers poses for *Picture Post* magazine in Normandy. He is equipped with a No. 4 Mark I rifle, 1937 webbing, Light Service respirator and Verey pistol. (IWM B 9005)

Above right:
The Mark III 'turtleback' infantry helmet, issued in 1944 in time for D-Day, was intended to give more protection to the sides and back of the head.

Left:
The Light Service respirator, first issued in 1941, but first seeing widespread use in northern Europe.

The cap badge of the Parachute Regiment, with a pair of jump qualification wings in the background.

insignia. Standard battledress was worn by most, but more often than not a relaxed style of dress was adopted. The standard issue woollen pullover was often preferred, together with the undistinguished-looking woollen 'cap, comforter' worn as the standard Commando headdress in action, by Army Commandos at least, until the issue of the familiar green beret in 1943.

All Commandos were specifically trained in stealth and close combat at Achnacarry; they were to be instructed in the use of the knife for silent killing, and would need specialist tools to carry out their trade. Captains William Ewart Fairburn and Eric Anthony Sykes, formerly officers in the Shanghai Police and later recruited to the army, developed their Fairburn-Sykes knife from their experiences on the tough Shanghai waterfront. The knife was formally adopted for use by all special forces (including Commandos, the Special Air Service – itself developed from No. 2 Commando – and the Parachute Regiment). There are many versions, housed in a leather scabbard with distinctive tabs that were supposed to be sewn securely to the uniform.

Like the Commandos that had spawned them, paratroopers were intended to be self-sufficient, lightly armed and with the minimum equipment, as they were often dropped behind enemy lines and had to await reinforcement. At the suggestion of General Browning, the Red Beret was adopted as the distinctive headdress of the Parachute Regiment from the outset in August 1942. Parachute Qualification Wings ('jump wings') were awarded from early 1941 (approved in

December 1940) to all men who had passed through the Parachute Training School at Ringway, near Manchester.

Although paratroopers were given standard 1937 pattern webbing equipment and battledress, they were nevertheless identifiable by some specific items of uniform and equipment. Distinctive were the paratrooper battledress trousers, supplied with larger pockets and a special inset pocket for the Fairburn-Sykes fighting knife. Even more distinctive was the camouflaged 'smock' – designated the 'Smock, Denison (Parachute Troops)' – that was to provide both weatherproofing and camouflage and was worn over battledress. To protect the head, a special type of helmet was worn, designated 'Helmet, steel, airborne troops'. This type of helmet was adopted in 1942, and was worn in combat, as well as during jumping.

Associated with Commandos and paratroopers alike, but used widely throughout the British Army, was the Sten sub-machine gun (or machine carbine in British service), first adopted in 1941. In 1939, the British Army had no effective sub-machine gun. After Dunkirk, the effectiveness of this type of weapon in close combat was realised and an order was placed for M1928 Thompson sub-machine guns from the USA. The Thompson was a complex and beautifully engineered piece of equipment, but something that could be mass-produced by unskilled labour was more urgently required. The Sten provided the solution: effectively a steel tube containing the bolt and acting as a shroud for the barrel. Much of the manufacture was carried out by stamping (rather than machining) to keep the production simple, and was carried out in a great many small workshops the length and breadth of

Below left:
The Sten machine carbine; easily manufactured by small businesses, it was often assembled by women.

Below right:
The second pattern Fairburn-Sykes fighting knife, as used by Commandos, Paratroopers and other Special Forces.

ONE MAN'S WAR: PRIVATE VICTOR MORRIS

Private Morris was a driver of a universal 'Bren' carrier with the Somerset Light Infantry, serving with the 43rd Wessex Division in Europe. He was called up to the Royal Fusiliers in May 1940; assigned to the 80th Division, located in Western Command, Fusilier Morris's brigade was the junior one of the Division. Within the 80th, Victor Morris trained as a Bren carrier driver, and instructed in the operation of the Bren light machine gun, gaining skills he would take with him during his subsequent reassignment to the 43rd Wessex Division, one of the key follow-up divisions in the battle for Normandy in 1944. Victor Morris was to take part in the battles around Caen in July 1944, particularly the struggle for Hill 112 on 10 July 1944. Commanding the south-western approach to the city, the Hill blocked the route to the open country, out of the *bocage* towards Falaise. Opposed by an SS Panzer battalion equipped with Tiger tanks, the men of the 43rd Wessex Division met strong resistance. Private Morris survived the assault and took part in the liberation of northern Europe by Monty's 21st Army Group. As in all previous wars, the accumulation of battle souvenirs was an inevitable consequence of being in action; Private Morris accumulated daggers and Nazi insignia to bring home. He would be granted special leave two days after the end of the war – to mark his birthday.

Above: Nazi battle souvenirs collected by Private Morris in 1944–5.

Left: Private Victor Morris of the Somerset Light Infantry in northern Europe.

Britain and Canada, often assembled by women. The Sten was cheaply made and total production ran to in excess of four million; it was a valuable and effective weapon.

The PIAT (Projector, Infantry, Anti-Tank) was a formidable weapon in capable hands. The PIAT was based on the spring-loaded spigot principle, in which the spring was to force the spigot (a steel canister and rod) into the base of the 3-pound projectile, a force that then ignited the charge, thereby propelling the projectile towards its target. This highly portable weapon (though weighing in excess of 30 pounds) was first introduced in 1942, replacing the cumbersome and obsolete Boys anti-tank rifle. Deploying the PIAT required nerve, as first cocking the weapon depended on 200 pounds of brute force acting against the spring system; discharging the projectile fortunately re-cocked the weapon for further use. Despite its drawbacks, the PIAT was effective (at a range of about 100 yards) against most tanks – as well as static fortifications.

The Projector, Infantry, Anti-Tank (PIAT) was a formidable weapon that relied upon a spring-loaded spigot to launch a hollow point charge. It took immense strength to cock the weapon, and considerable nerve to use it.

SUGGESTED READING

Anon. *Britain's Modern Army*. Odham's Press, c. 1943.

Badsey, S. *D-Day: From the Beaches of Normandy to the Liberation of France*. Tiger, 1994.

Bouchery, J. *The British Soldier from D-Day to VE Day, Volume 1. Uniforms, Insignia, Equipments*. Histoire & Collections, 1998.

Bouchery, J. *The British Soldier from D-Day to VE day, Volume 2. Organisation, Armament, Tanks and Vehicles*. Histoire & Collections, 1999.

Brayley, M. J., and Chappell, M. *The British Army 1939–45 (1) North-West Europe*. Osprey, 2001.

Brayley, M. J., and Chappell, M. *The British Army 1939–45 (2) Middle East & Mediterranean*. Osprey, 2002.

Brayley, M. J., and Chappell, M. *The British Army 1939–45 (3) The Far East*. Osprey, 2002.

Brayley, M. J., and Ingram, R. *The World War II Tommy: British Army Uniforms, European Theatre 1939–45 in Colour Photographs*. Crowood, 1998.

Brayley, M. J., and Ingram, R. *Khaki Drill & Jungle Green: British Tropical Uniforms 1939–45 in Colour Photographs*. Crowood, 2000.

Davies, B. *British Army Uniforms and Insignia of WWII*. Arms & Armour Press, 1983.

Doyle, P. *Prisoner of War in Germany*. Shire, 2008.

Doyle, P., and Evans, P. *The Home Front: British Wartime Memorabilia*. Crowood, 2007.

Doyle, P., and Evans, P. *The British Soldier in Europe, 1939–1945*. Crowood, 2009.

Forty, G. *British Army Handbook 1939–1945*. Chancellor Press, 2000.

Fraser, D. *And We Shall Shock Them: The British Army in the Second World War*. Hodder & Stoughton, 1983.

Glenn, H. *For King and Country: British Airborne Uniforms, Insignia & Equipment in World War II*. Schiffer, 1999.

Gordon, D. B. *Equipment of the WWII Tommy*. Pictorial Histories Publishing, 2004.

Gordon, D. B. *Weapons of the WWII Tommy*. Pictorial Histories Publishing, 2004.

Gordon, D. B. *Uniforms of the WWII Tommy*. Pictorial Histories Publishing, 2005.

Hastings, M. *The British Army. The Definitive History of the Twentieth Century*. Cassell, 2007.

Hay, I. *Arms and the Men*. HMSO, 1950.

Linklater, E. *The Campaign in Italy*. HMSO, 1951.

Mackenzie, S. P. *The Home Guard*. Oxford University Press, 1996.

Moreman, T. *British Commandos 1940–46*. Osprey, 2006.

North, J. *N.-W. Europe 1944–45*. HMSO, 1953.

Sheppard, E. W. *Britain at War: The Army, British and Allies from July 1943 to September 1944*. Hutchinson, *c*. 1945.

Sheppard, E. W. *Britain at War. The Army, British and Allies from October 1944 to May 1945*. Hutchinson, *c*. 1945.

Smurthwaite, D., Nicholls, M., and Washington, L. *'Against All Odds': The British Army of 1939–40*. National Army Museum, 1990.

INDEX